THE STRESS POCKETBOOK

2nd Edition

By Mary Richards

Drawings by Phil Hailstone

D1390430

"Excellent. To the point. Practical. A vital tool for everyone who wants to reduce their stress at work."
Adam Allen, Principal Engineer, Railways, Scott Wilson Group plc

"This is a little gem, brimming full of insights and practical tips for recognising, controlling and relieving stress. With stress reaching epidemic levels in our modern world, we can all benefit from this book's guidance and direction."
Dr. Alison Salt, Consultant Paediatrician,
Great Ormond Street Hospital for Children, London

Published by:
Management Pocketbooks Ltd
Laurel House, Station Approach, Alresford, Hants SO24 9JH, U.K.
Tel: +44 (0)1962 735573 Fax: +44 (0)1962 733637
Email: sales@pocketbook.co.uk
Website: www.pocketbook.co.uk

First published 1998. This edition published 2009. Reprinted 2011.
ISBN: 978 1 906610 09 8

E-book ISBN: 978 1 908284 15 0

British Library Cataloguing-in-Publication Data – A catalogue record for this book is available from the British Library.

Design, typesetting and graphics by **efex ltd**. Printed in U.K.

CONTENTS

INTRODUCTION

WORK & PRESSURE GO HAND IN HAND

There are:

- Deadlines to meet
- Mistakes to rectify
- Demands to satisfy
- Targets to achieve
- Problems to resolve
- Challenges to rise to

You may find:

- Goal posts are moved
- Work is interrupted
- Working relationships become strained
- There is too much or too little to do
- The work stretches you or bores you
- The future of your job is uncertain

Everyone in every job experiences pressure.

TOO MUCH PRESSURE

Too much pressure for
too long leads to **Stress...**

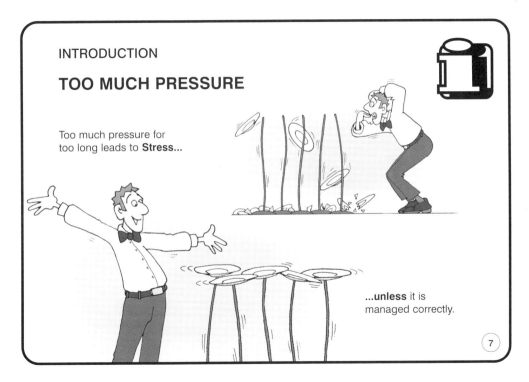

...unless it is
managed correctly.

PRESSURE LEVELS

At one level, pressure may be a positive aid to performance:

- The deadline that spurs you on
- The target that motivates you
- The challenge that inspires you

PRESSURE LEVELS

At another level, pressure may trigger a mechanism to tell you that something is wrong and you start to experience stress.

Continue beyond this level for too long and you can seriously damage your mental and physical well-being.

REALITY OF THE WORLD WE WORK IN

As technology...

- Reshapes jobs
- Increases the speed at which we work
- Makes information and knowledge quickly out of date

...we will all experience more pressure at work.

As markets...

- Demand a more flexible workforce
- Influence the shape of organisations
- Remove the 'job for life'

...we will all experience more pressure at work.

YOU CAN CHOOSE

As the pressure at work increases you have a choice:

Learn how to manage it ...

YOU CAN CHOOSE

... or let work pressures manage you!

STRESS

A DEFINITION OF STRESS

Because stress means different things to different people...

- Tackling a task for the first time
- A meeting with the boss
- Giving a presentation
- A delayed delivery of important supplies
- An irate customer
- A tight deadline
- An unnecessary mistake
- A difference of opinion

...because what's stressful to you today, may not necessarily be stressful to you tomorrow or the day after...

A DEFINITION OF STRESS

...because stress can be...

POSITIVE or **NEGATIVE**

POSITIVE	NEGATIVE
An opportunity to prove yourself	You become less efficient – performance and productivity fall
You work better to a deadline	Deadlines send you into a blind panic – you achieve nothing
It gives you a positive emotional charge or 'high'	You seek comfort by snacking, smoking or drinking

...stress is best described as: **an individual's response to pressure.**

WHAT HAPPENS INSIDE YOUR BODY?

If you perceive a pressure as a threat or a challenge, your body will automatically go into overdrive:

- Your heart rate increases and your blood pressure rises
- Your muscles harden and tense in readiness for action
- Your digestive process slows and more acid is produced in the stomach
- Your breathing becomes quicker as your lungs try to take up more oxygen

This automatic reaction is often known as the 'fight' or 'flight' response because these changes prepare the body to be able to fight or run away.

USEFUL CYCLE OR DOWNWARD SPIRAL?

The fight or flight response was a very appropriate mechanism for primitive man. Being able to fight or run to safety when under pressure ensured his survival.
It was a useful cycle.

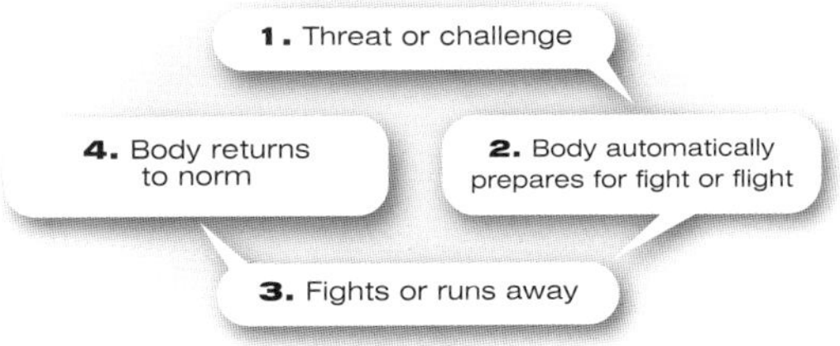
1. Threat or challenge
2. Body automatically prepares for fight or flight
3. Fights or runs away
4. Body returns to norm

However, try applying this cycle to your work environment.

You feel threatened or challenged by pressures at work. The fight or flight response is triggered. Your body goes into overdrive. Neither fighting nor running away does much for your career prospects. So you don't. You are now under more pressure both mentally and physically. You continue to ignore the fight or flight cycle and, as a consequence, the pressures increase. You have unwittingly converted a useful cycle into a downward spiral.

THE TRIGGER

The key to understanding and managing stress is to know that the fight or flight response is only activated when you perceive a pressure as a threat or challenge. Think about it:

Your boss asks you to meet in Room 4 in half an hour. **If** your response is to start to think...

- What have I done wrong?
- Am I going to be fired?
- Why Room 4?
- Why me?

...you will trigger the fight or flight response. You become so concerned about the meeting that you can think of little else. Consequently, you waste half an hour and in doing so increase the pressure on yourself. You will arrive at the meeting in a state of stress.

SOURCE OF STRESS

There are many pressures at work, but there is only one source of stress. **You.**

Check it out for yourself. Think of a stressful situation at work. Ask yourself the following questions:

- What is creating the pressure in this situation?
- What is the response to the pressure in this situation?
- Who is responding?
- Where, therefore, is the source of stress?

Because stress is an individual's response to pressure, you will always be the source of your own stress. Your stress will be the result of your own response to the pressures you experience at work.

WHERE MIGHT PRESSURES AT WORK COME FROM?

The physical environment: noise; overcrowding; uncomfortable working conditions; lack of parking facilities...

The characteristics of the job: repetitive work; tight deadlines; shift work; too much or too little to do; too much or too little responsibility; travel; long or anti-social hours; responding to emergencies...

The organisation's culture: being in a minority (male/female; smoking/non-smoking; etc); rules, regulations and expectations; level of stability or tendency to change...

The people (management, staff, suppliers, customers, shareholders, you): relationships with others at work; not being the right person for the job; being too demanding of yourself and others; being a 'yes' person; being a dinosaur; inefficient work habits...

HOW TO RECOGNISE STRESS

Your response to a pressure may result in stress, but how will you recognise it? Although physiologically we all react in a similar way (rise in heart rate, tense muscles, etc) our overt reactions and behaviours may be very different. These are just a few of the many signs you might see, hear or feel:

- **SEE:** nail biting; twitching eye/eyebrow; frequent licking or biting of lips; excessive blinking; a change in eating or drinking patterns from abstinence to over-indulgence; signs of tiredness; crying...
- **HEAR:** slamming of doors, phones, papers or fists on desks; unusually rapid speech; drumming of fingers; emotional outbursts; swearing; unco-ordinated speech; jingling of coins or keys; pen top flicking; sighing...
- **FEEL:** sweaty; clammy; flushed; tense; frustrated; angry; isolated; hopeless; impatient; irritable; depressed; anxious; stretched; challenged...

HEED SIGNS OF STRESS

Stress is a downward spiral that can seriously damage your mental and physical well-being.

Fortunately, your body will give you signs that you are stressed. These signs are the results of your thoughts and responses to pressure. **Heed them.**

YOUR THOUGHTS

THE FACTS

When your thoughts trigger stress, your body responds:

'I can't possibly stand up in front of those people'

You break out in a cold sweat

'The boss will kill me if I don't get it finished by tonight'

Your stomach begins to churn

Controlling your thoughts will help you to control your responses. This will reduce your stress.

YOUR THOUGHTS

THE PROOF & CONSEQUENCES

Prove to yourself that your body responds to your thoughts. Watch a film or read a book. If the story is frightening, you may feel your pulse racing. If the story is sad, the tears may start to flow.

Now consider the consequences of this at work. If, for example, you really think that you're going to lose your job, your body will start to behave as though you've already lost it.

How do your thoughts affect your behaviour at work? Are they generating pressure and stress, or are they reducing it?

THE NATURE OF THOUGHTS

Thoughts can be negative. Thoughts can be positive. They behave in a manner that like attracts like. Negative thoughts attract more negative thoughts:

- *I'll never get this report finished in time; It really is a hopeless situation; I simply can't make head nor tail of it; time is running out*

And positive thoughts attract more positive thoughts:

- *Things are definitely on a roll today; I've already made good headway with my list of tasks; there have been very few interruptions and I'm really feeling on top of things*

Negative thoughts **increase** the pressure. Positive thoughts **reduce** it.

THE NATURE OF THOUGHTS

Thoughts can be fleeting, intermittent, persistent, or life-long friends. The longer you hold a thought, the stronger it gets. As a result, thoughts can become:

- Self-fulfilling:
  ✗ I doubt if I'll get the job; I'm sure there will be someone better qualified than me…
  ✗ I bet I'll be late for the meeting; the journey to that venue is always a nightmare…
  ✔ I feel certain that I can improve on the situation; there's often another approach
- Or the basis for a firm belief:
  ✗ My voice is never heard; ever since I was a child…
  ✗ I'm no good at working to deadlines; the very thought of it grips me with fear…
  ✔ I'm a great team player; I always get to work with the most inspiring people

What long-term thoughts are you holding on to?
Are they generating or reducing pressure?

THOUGHTS & FEELINGS

Thoughts cause feelings. They can drag you down:

- If only I was more organised – *you feel dissatisfied*
- How many more times do we have to go through this – *you feel exasperated*
- That's it. I've had enough of this – *you feel angry*

Or lift you up:

- That's one of the best pieces of work I've done – *you feel pleased*
- I'm really looking forward to my new job – *you feel excited*
- I got so much out of that workshop. It was truly inspirational – *you feel delighted*

How are you feeling now? Why? What are you thinking? Are your thoughts negative or positive? Are they fresh thoughts, or old friends? Are they making you feel better or are they making you feel worse?

THE WAY IT FEELS

Feelings. For some people, the very word brings on stress. Feelings are a vast scale of emotions that can range from despair, guilt, rage and blame, through frustration and irritation, into hopefulness, delight, joy and appreciation.

Feelings are your gauge. A gauge that tells you whether things are 'good' or 'bad', 'better' or 'worse'.

When the feelings are good, hold on to them; nurse them and feed them. Encourage them to grow. Let them lift you.

When the feelings are 'bad' let them go. Change your thoughts. Switch your focus. Bring on a better feeling.

YOUR THOUGHTS

THE WAY YOU SEE IT

Thoughts influence perceptions. They act as a personal lens through which you view life. Your lens allows you to:

- Magnify
  - a small success as a significant triumph
  - a minor incident as a major crisis
- Travel through time
  - to envisage a successful result
  - or predict the worst possible outcome

THE WAY YOU SEE IT

Your lens lets you:

- Adjust the contrast
  – to give a rosier view
  – or to remove all the silver linings from your black clouds

- Filter according to taste
  – you're pleased that your colleague has been promoted
  – or you're incensed that you didn't secure the job for yourself

Your lens creates your perception. Refocus it to give thoughts that create a less stressful view.

A SITUATION & AN EXPERIENCE

Thoughts, feelings and perceptions form a cycle of influence. Together they combine to form your perspective and your experience.

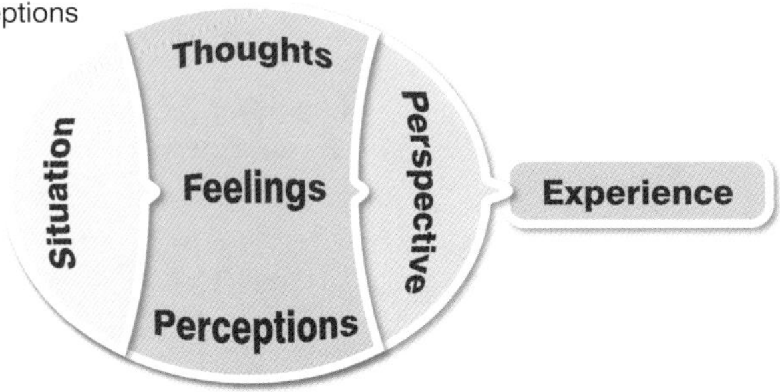

People on a plane, travelling at the same time in the same space to the same destination, will all have a different experience. An experience is unique to an individual. It is a personal creation made from thoughts, feelings and perceptions. The situation is just the situation. But because you can adjust your thoughts, feelings and perceptions, the experience is what you choose to make it.

PERSPECTIVES INFLUENCE RESULTS

Some perspectives generate stress. Others don't.

Imagine that a new software program is going to be installed on your computer at work. You might think:

- New software probably means job losses – *you feel worried*
- It'll take me twice as long to get the work done – *you feel frustrated*
- Thank goodness the company's joining the 21st century – *you feel relieved*
- Great, it's an opportunity to add another skill to my CV – *you feel enthusiastic*

How you respond to a pressure depends on your choice of perspective.

INFLUENCE & CHOICE

Your perspective may be influenced by:

- Previous experience of a situation; did you survive, how did you manage then?
- Being faced with something for the first time; fear of the unknown, no previous experience to draw on
- What else is going on in your life; nothing much or the straw that breaks the camel's back
- How you feel at that particular time; on top of the world or positively steam rollered
- Whether you are alone or supported by others; being isolated or being able to share your concerns
- Your beliefs and values; that people should be treated equally, that your home life is more important than your work
- Your personality; type A (competitive, high achieving, restless) or type B (more easy going, more relaxed)

Your perspective may be influenced, but you are still free to make choices. Who tells you whether to laugh at a joke or not? You may be influenced, but the choice is yours.

THE RELIEF OF CHANGING YOUR THOUGHTS

When your experience is creating too much pressure, try:

- Changing your thoughts
- Adjusting your perception
- Finding a way to feel better about the situation

It doesn't matter which approach you take. Your thoughts, feelings and perceptions are all interlinked. Change one and you will influence the others. It's like a wheel: turn it and you will gain momentum.

Making a change doesn't require you to spin from 'loathing' a situation to 'loving' it in one move. You only need to make a change that brings an improvement to your experience. Turn the wheel. Experience the relief.

CHOOSING YOUR PERSPECTIVE

Learning to adjust and choose pressure-reducing thoughts and perspectives may take a little practice.

- Generate different perspectives by:
  - **Writing** the facts of the situation down on paper; it will clarify your thinking and help you to see the situation in different ways
  - **Checking** your lens (see pages 30 and 31). Are you magnifying the best or the worst aspects of the situation? Are you dealing with the present moment, regretting the past, or fearing the future? Adjust your lens to give you a better view
  - **Putting** yourself in the shoes of others. How might they perceive the situation?
  - **Talking** to others. Other people will always be able to help you find a different perspective. You don't have to agree with them, but they may open your mind to even more ideas
- Assess each perspective in terms of whether it will generate more or less pressure
- Choose the perspective that will reduce your pressure

PUTTING IT IN PERSPECTIVE

When you can only think of perspectives that increase the pressure:

- **Imagine the worst.** Think how the situation might be worse than it really is. It will enable you to view your original thoughts in a better light and it will put you under less pressure. Try it. Things will not be as bad as they seemed at first
- **Consider someone else.** There will always be someone whose situation is more challenging than yours. Thinking of others can help you focus on things that you're really grateful for
- **Remember the transient nature of life.** The moon waxes and wanes; the tide flows in and out; the seasons come and go. There is a time for everything and everything changes. Nothing in life is forever
- **Check your values.** Are you becoming stressed about something that, in the bigger picture of life, is not all that significant? What's really important to you in life? Don't stress yourself with less important things

BEYOND YOUR CONTROL?

Rumours of redundancy, company take-overs and changes in business legislation are all situations where you may be under pressure because you **feel** that you have no control. You blame the management, the system or fate. Your thoughts confirm your helplessness. They generate stress.

Don't concern yourself with things that are out of your control. Focus instead on what is within your control. If, for example, you think you might be made redundant, make sure that given the choice the company would want to keep you; get your CV up to date, study and practise interview techniques.

In every situation there is always something within your control. Start with controlling your thoughts. They will deliver controlled responses.

CONTROLLING YOUR THOUGHTS

When you are under pressure you may find that:

- You can't think straight
- You can't focus on the job in hand
- Your thoughts run away with you

The moment you recognise that your thoughts have taken over, you can start to regain control. Listening to your thoughts feeds them. If you don't like what you hear, stop listening. Change the channel and tune into something else. You might choose to:

- Switch your focus to a wonderful picture, a beautiful object or a fabulous view
- Recite a funny poem
- Talk about something you're passionate about
- Generate a ridiculous amount of appreciation for the smallest of things
- Do something that completely absorbs you
- Actively seek silence

Whatever action you decide to take, the sooner you take it the easier it will be to stay in control. Be as persistent in your efforts as your thoughts are with you.

VOICING YOUR THOUGHTS

Thoughts are reinforced by words. Whether written or spoken, words give life to your thoughts, so consider them carefully. To keep your stress levels low try:

- **Listening to your language**: if it's heavy (impossible; devastating; diabolical…) try energising it (fantastic; amazing; wonderful…). When circumstances allow, relax your voice with a cheery whistle or gentle hum. Sing
- **Cleaning up your act**: if you can't find anything constructive to say, say nothing
- **Self-talk**: repeat positive thoughts over and over to yourself. Choose words that ring true for you and let them draw you towards better feelings
- **Saying it out loud**: share your positive thoughts with others – it will strengthen your resolve to be positive. It will help you all to feel better

Putting your thoughts into words helps to make your thoughts a reality, so choose your words with care. Thoughts create your experiences and influence your responses.

YOUR RESPONSES

YOUR RESPONSE, YOUR STRESS, YOUR CHOICE

Realising that stress comes from your thoughts and responses can be quite sobering. However, it can also be liberating:

- You can choose your thoughts and responses; you may be influenced, but ultimately the choice is yours
- You can control your thoughts and responses; it may take effort, time and even practice, but they are yours to control

Exercise this choice. Take control. Reduce your stress.

RESPONDING TO PRESSURE

Responses to pressure vary from person to person and from pressure to pressure. They may depend on what else is actually happening at the time or how you're feeling.

Amongst others, your response may be:

Physical – 'butterflies' in your stomach, headaches, shallow breathing...

Mental – forgetfulness, lack of concentration, worry...

Emotional – quarrelsome, defensive, embarrassed...

Behavioural – too busy for anything other than working, drinking/smoking more than usual, insomnia...

How do **you** respond to the pressures at work? Use some of the ideas on the following pages to help control your responses to the pressures of time, workload, change, people, conflict and you.

PRESSURE OF TIME

Time is one of the greatest pressures at work. How do you respond to it?

- Not enough time *(panic)*
- Wasted time *(annoyance; guilt)*
- Interrupted time *(frustration; impatience)*
- Not giving enough time *(concern; worry)*
- Not being on time *(anxiety)*
- Too much time *(boredom)*

These responses are all signs of stress. You may experience them many times in each day.

YOUR RESPONSES

PRESSURE OF TIME

MAKING IT WORSE

You will always be under a certain amount of pressure from time because it's a limited resource. But do you make the pressure worse than it need be? Do you:

- Always stop what you're doing to help others?
- Open the post or your e-mail as soon as it arrives?
- Work to unrealistic deadlines?
- Spend a disproportionate amount of time dotting the i's and crossing the t's?
- Watch the clock?
- Write and rewrite lengthy 'To Do' lists?
- Under-estimate the time you need?
- Work through the day without any breaks?
- Busy yourself with the tasks that interest or flatter you?
- Arrive late for meetings?
- Spend most of your day dealing with phone calls and other interruptions?
- Allow one delay at the beginning of your day to snowball into your whole schedule so that you end up chasing your tail?

Doing any of these things will increase the pressure you're under.

YOUR RESPONSES

PRESSURE OF TIME

WAYS TO REDUCE THE PRESSURE

Try reducing the pressure you're under by:

- Applying the Pareto principle to your list of tasks (20% of the tasks will give you 80% of your results); identify those key tasks and make them a priority
- Distinguishing between urgent tasks (crisis, unplanned, demands, etc) and important tasks (that achieve your prime objectives, give you maximum return for effort)
- Being selective; not all tasks need 'polishing'

YOUR RESPONSES

PRESSURE OF TIME

WAYS TO REDUCE THE PRESSURE (Cont'd)

- Planning uninterrupted time; divert your phone; make it known that you are unavailable
- Saying 'no' to 'urgent' requests, interruptions and unreasonable demands
- Planning to do the most demanding tasks when you're at your best
- Setting realistic deadlines for tasks and sticking to them; when necessary, re-negotiate deadlines as soon as possible
- Working together; if you have the authority, delegate; alternatively, think about asking others for help; who would do your job if you were away?

PRESSURE OF WORK

When you've got too much or too little to do at work do you:

- Blame others?
- Complain, gripe or groan?
- Work every hour available or do nothing?
- Worry that you'll lose your job?

Negative thoughts and responses will only add to your pressure. They will take you down the spiral of stress. Try to stop them. Replace them with more constructive thoughts and responses.

YOUR RESPONSES

PRESSURE OF WORK

CONSTRUCTIVE RESPONSES

When you've got too much work, stop. Establish the real reason for your excessive workload. Maybe you need to:

- Plan ahead for known increases in workload (end of month duties; seasonal peaks; people on leave; etc)
- Start delegating or delegate more effectively
- Work more efficiently – renegotiate deadlines; only attend relevant meetings
- Balance your tasks – mix those you like with those you don't like; the long with the short; the difficult with the easy
- Focus on one task at a time
- Be more proactive rather than reactive
- Arrange to work off-site or from home if appropriate
- Talk to someone to get a different perspective and new ideas about how to manage your workload
- Stop worrying and start doing
- Put the tips on pages 46 and 47 into practice

WHEN THERE'S NOT ENOUGH TO DO

Try to:

- Look for ways to contribute. Who is rushed off their feet? How could you help them? Offer to do tasks that are well within your grasp – phone screening, photocopying, fetching and delivering. Helping out just once normally leads to work coming your way a second time
- Set yourself deadlines, goals and challenges to give yourself enough pressure to get moving. Perhaps you can do a task with greater accuracy than before
- Generate ideas on how to increase your workload by talking to others
- Check your job specification. Are you doing everything you're supposed to do? Discuss it with your boss

RESPONDING TO CHANGE

When faced with change you will go through the following process:

- **Awareness** How will this affect me?
- **Shock** They're going to do what? I can't believe it
- **Denial** There's no way this'll work. It'll blow over
- **Frustration** If it wasn't for the management...
- **Realisation** If that's what's going to happen then...
- **Acceptance** If you can't beat them, join them
- **Adaptation** It could be worse. At least it means that...
- **Integration** The change becomes the norm. There's nothing to react to

Regardless of the change, be it positive or negative, you will go through all of these stages. However, the speed at which you go through them will vary from change to change and from person to person.

RESPONDING TO CHANGE

REDUCING THE PRESSURE

All stages of the change process are likely to put you under pressure, but some more than others. To reduce the pressure try:

- Asking questions – seek as much information as possible; you may be rejecting the change before you understand the full story
- Being as open-minded as possible – for every negative you identify, find a positive
- Moving with the change as quickly as possible – while it is important to question change and not 'blindly' accept it, the quicker you move with rather than against it, the sooner pressure will be reduced
- Sharing your concerns with others – being alone with change will increase the pressure you're under; talking with others will help you see things from different perspectives

INTRODUCING CHANGE

When you introduce change to others, reduce the pressure they're under by:

- Giving them time to come to terms with the thought of change; avoid surprises
- Where possible, introducing the change as an idea, a topic for discussion rather than a fait accompli
- Involving them as much as possible at all stages of the change; if they are involved, they will own it and be more positive about the change
- Talking to them about how they feel; when people have a voice it gives them a sense of control, reducing the pressure they're under
- Giving them as much information as possible; stress is often caused by people drawing their own conclusions through lack of information

RESPONDING TO PEOPLE

- The customer is always right
- Seniors must be heeded
- Colleagues must be co-operated with

Responding to people at work can put you under pressure. Try not to let your behaviour make it any worse. Aggressive (fight) and submissive (flight) behaviour will both increase the pressure.

Use assertive behaviour instead. Learn to:

- Say 'no' to unreasonable requests and demands
- Reduce the pressure of conflict

RESPONDING TO PEOPLE

SAYING 'YES' WHEN YOU MEAN 'NO'

When...

- Everyone wants everything done yesterday
- Your day is just one interruption after another
- You feel that you're always 'fire-fighting'
- Your tasks remain untouched, while you deal with tasks for others

...you need to be proactive and say 'no'.

If you find it difficult to say 'no' try the **ADO** technique:

Acknowledge	show that you understand the request: 'So you want me to put the figures into a table that you can use in your presentation tomorrow?'
Decline	with a reason, but you don't have to explain yourself: 'I can do it, but not right now...'
Offer	an alternative: 'I can do it first thing tomorrow morning.'

RESPONDING BY PLACING BLAME

Blame is a popular response to many of the pressures you face at work:

- You didn't get promoted, so you blame your boss
- You feel insecure in your job, so you blame the management
- You're late for a meeting, so you blame the previous one – it over-ran

Blame is an attempt to deflect the focus away from yourself. You use it when you feel threatened, insecure, alienated, out of control in some way. You use it when you're stressed. But it doesn't help.

RESPONDING BY PLACING BLAME

In some situations, blame may bring you temporary relief from pressure in the short-term. It might, for example, 'buy you time' or turn the focus temporarily away from you. Perhaps you'll feel better pointing the finger at someone else and letting yourself off the hook. The relief is momentary. Having placed blame, you now have more pressures to contend with.

If you've used blame to:

- Cover a mistake, you worry that you may yet be found out
- Abdicate responsibility, it confirms your lack of control

If you want to avoid an increase in pressure, don't place blame.

YOUR RESPONSES

RESPONDING WITH A GRIMACE

When you're asked to:

- Do a task you don't want to do
- Work with someone you don't want to work with
- Be in an environment you'd rather not be in

do you respond by…

- Grimacing (secretly or publicly)
- Instigating a group gripe

or do you take a deep breath and resolve to find a positive approach to the situation?

Grimacing and griping will only increase the pressure. Finding something to feel positive about will reduce it.

GIVING IT YOUR BEST SHOT

There will always be times when you'd rather not do something, but for whatever reason, you just have to. At times like these you can:

- Approach the task with resistance, making it quite clear by your actions that it's the last thing you want to do
- Be consumed with inertia

Your negative approach will affect you, the task, and those around you.

Alternatively, before you start the task, shift your perspective from 'I have to and don't want to' to 'I don't mind and I can see benefits in doing so'. Use the tips from pages 30 to 38 to help you. If you're not doing a job that you love, at least try to find things to love about the job that you're doing. Giving something your best shot will make you feel good about yourself. Try it.

RESPONDING TO CONFLICT

When you experience conflict at work do you:

- Avoid bringing attention to it in the hope that it will go away?
- Ask those involved in the conflict how they see the situation?
- Use status, authority or seniority to get what you want?
- Keep to the facts of the situation and avoid becoming emotional?
- Love it when you win and hate it when you lose?
- Select the best solution for everyone, or the solution you prefer?

The way you choose to deal with a conflict will determine how much stress it generates. Check your thoughts and responses. Do you increase the pressure when you deal with conflict or reduce it?

RESPONDING TO CONFLICT

INCREASING THE PRESSURE

Conflicts at work arise because there is a difference – a difference of opinion, personality, objectives, interest, values, viewpoints and so on.

If you think of conflict in terms of a fight, a struggle, winners and losers, you may become defensive, aggressive, try to ignore it, or walk away from it. These are all classic responses associated with stress.

Take a winners and losers approach to conflict and the losers will always:

- Have a desire for revenge
- Be inclined to bear a grudge

A winners and losers approach will simply encourage further conflict. There will always be a 'sore point'. It will fester. It will reappear.

RESPONDING TO CONFLICT

REDUCING THE PRESSURE

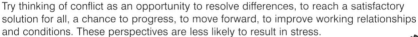

Try thinking of conflict as an opportunity to resolve differences, to reach a satisfactory solution for all, a chance to progress, to move forward, to improve working relationships and conditions. These perspectives are less likely to result in stress.

Take a win/win approach to conflict and you will reduce or eliminate pressure because:

- Everyone has a chance to be heard
- Working relationships and conditions are improved
- More trust and respect are generated
- Future conflicts become easier to confront

RESPONDING TO CONFLICT

THE LEAST STRESSFUL APPROACH

1. Acknowledge that conflict exists. Ignore it at an early stage and it will be much harder to resolve later.
2. Understand everyone's position. Listen to what is said. Restate each position to show that you've understood.
3. Identify key issues and concerns. Encourage honesty.
4. Search for possible solutions. Be creative. Be open minded. Don't evaluate or judge at this stage.
5. Select the best solution for everyone, not the solution you prefer.
6. Implement the solution and re-check that everyone is satisfied. If not, conflict will recur.

Always use language that is factual and neutral. Avoid emotion and blame.

This process is a series of stages. Each stage must be complete before moving on to the next one. Don't be in too much of a hurry. Haste might result in things being overlooked, people not being heard, people not having enough time to search deeply and to be honest.

RESPONDING TO THE TRUE PRESSURE

When you realise that you're stressed and that you need to control your thoughts and responses to a pressure, make sure that you focus on the true pressure. Think carefully about it:

- Is your colleague really irritating you or are you actually concerned about your impending appraisal?
- Were you really so angry that the coffee machine wasn't working or was it just the last straw after a difficult meeting?
- Perhaps the pressure isn't even at work. Maybe it's at home and it just comes with you every day
- Or, maybe the true pressure is you?

PUTTING YOURSELF UNDER PRESSURE

You put yourself under pressure when you:

- Constantly strive for perfection
- Always put the needs of others first
- Lack self-esteem
- Take things personally
- Blame others for your situation
- Dislike your job, but stay in it out of habit
- Try to please people all the time
- Need to be 'right'
- Say 'yes' every time you're asked to do something
- Carry your responsibilities all the time – never switching off

PUTTING YOURSELF UNDER PRESSURE

Try not to be so hard on yourself, and others. Reduce the pressure. You don't have to change your personality, just ease up a little from time to time.

Alternatively, you could say: 'That's just the way I am', 'I've always been like that', 'It's in my nature'. You could just carry on putting yourself under these pressures for the rest of your life.

Your pressure. Your response. Your choice. Your life.

Your lifestyle

LIVING WITH PRESSURE

Stress puts your body under pressure. It puts a strain on your heart and your digestive system. You become too busy or too tired to exercise or to eat a balanced diet. You haven't got time to relax and you really don't want anyone else to know that you're buckling under the pressure of work.

The way you lead your life can make you more resilient to the pressures of work. Or it can make the pressures worse.

YOUR VIEW OF LIFE

Your view of life shapes your experiences and affects your resilience to pressure.

Do you consider life to be an uphill struggle, or a journey to be enjoyed? Is it a gift or a burden? Are you on a treadmill, or a merry-go-round? Are you pessimistic or optimistic?

Do you bemoan the past: if only I'd had a better education; been born into a different family…? Or do you fear the future: I'll never be able to afford to retire; I don't know what I'll do if I lose my job…?

Are you living 'now' or are you planning to do that 'later' – when the children have left home; things ease off at work; you retire…

One of the most cost effective lifestyle changes that you can make, is to adjust your approach to life.

- Where it is negative, switch it to positive
- When it's about 'then' and 'when', change it to 'now'

A negative view can quite literally cost you your life.

THE ROLES YOU PLAY

Life is full of different roles. You may be:

- A hero to the child whose bike you fixed
- A menace to the driver you tailgated on the way home from work
- An angel to the old lady you helped across the road

Your life is full of roles because your life is just a story. Some roles you've chosen for yourself, some you've allowed others (parents; partners; siblings; colleagues...) to choose for you. Your life story is important because from it you create your own personal reality. You can create a story that's stress-full or stress-free.

YOUR LIFE STORY

Study your life story carefully. Does it make for easy living? Have you cast yourself in the best possible role? Life presents plenty of challenging situations over which you have no control, but as the script writer of your life, you dictate how those situations unfold. You choose your own role and you cast the roles of others. It's powerful stuff. Make sure you choose the most stress-free options! Refuse to play the victim and you remove the need to cast someone as a bully. Refrain from seeing yourself as the underdog and you don't need to wait to be rescued.

When you need to reduce the pressure in your life, examine your story closely. Re-script your life, change your roles, and enjoy yourself. You know that life is not a rehearsal.

THE BALANCING ACT

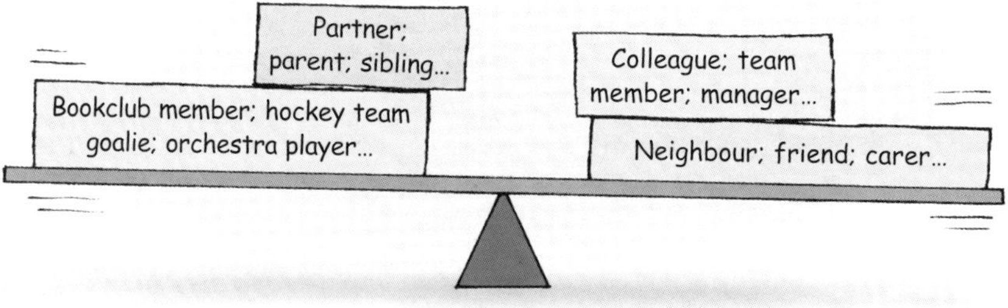

Juggling your many life roles can be demanding, but developing a healthy work/life balance will make you more resilient to pressure and stress.

'All work and no play...' is a common enough saying, but how seriously do you take it? How much leisure time do you allow yourself? What do you balance your working life with? When did you last 'play'?

PLANNING A BALANCED LIFE

To create a strong work-life balance, focus on the four areas of 'self', 'family', 'career' and 'community'. Identify desires and goals, and plan their achievement. For example:

SELF

- Find a way to bring music into my life
- Become fitter and slimmer

FAMILY

- Make one night a week 'family' night
- Find out more about our family history

CAREER

- Attend a course that will improve my skill level
- Seek opportunities for promotion

COMMUNITY

- Become involved in a fundraising activity
- Organise one aspect of the neighbourhood street party

An annual overview like this might be supported by a monthly plan, a weekly action list, or a daily diary. A little thought spent in this way will bring your life into focus. Your life will become more balanced and rewarding because your energy will be directed towards what is important for you right here and right now.

BEING PRESENT

Being fully present wherever you are and whatever you're doing will make you more resilient to pressure.

When you're at work, be at work. When you're at the gym, be at the gym. When you're at home, be at home. Leave your work at work. Park it. Drop it. Let it go.

Live life as it happens. Learn to 'be'. Concerning yourself with anything other than what's here and now will drain your precious energy. Your energy is vital to your well-being. Boost it as often as you can: keep your life clutter-free; appreciate what is around you; relax; laugh lots; eat healthily; and take regular exercise.

REGULAR EXERCISE

What happens when you see the words 'regular exercise'? Do you:

- Feel guilty because you know you should but...?
- Think you should turn to the next section because you're not the sporty kind?
- Think of exercise you used to enjoy before your life became so busy?
- Recall unhappy games lessons at school?
- Have visions of people who aren't at all like you?

You don't have to become a fitness fanatic, but you can build your defences against stress by improving your fitness.

IMPROVING YOUR FITNESS

To improve your fitness, focus on the level, frequency and type of exercise.

Level and frequency of exercise

- Aim for a gradual steady improvement; if you don't walk anywhere, start walking
- **Build up** to at least 30 minutes of moderate intensity exercise on 5 or more days a week. If you are starting from zero exercise, this will take several months to achieve. Don't expect too much of yourself too soon. A steady progression delivers results

Frequency of exercise

- Too much exercise is as bad as too little

As your fitness improves and you exercise more often, include plenty of variety in your programme and avoid doing the same type of activity on consecutive days

IMPROVING YOUR FITNESS

Choose exercise that:

- You enjoy – exercise can be sociable or solitary, indoors or outdoors, at home or at a club
- Will increase your rate of breathing
- Is varied – sometimes swim, sometimes cycle, sometimes jog...
- Is not competitive to the point that it increases stress and defeats the object entirely!
- You can fit into your already busy life. Yes, it will take effort, but too much effort and you'll stop. Think about:
  - using the stairs at work
  - walking the block at lunch time
  - walking up the escalator
  - cycling to work
  - getting off the bus a little earlier and walking the last 15 minutes home in the evenings

WHICH EXCUSE DO YOU USE?

Perhaps you:

- Haven't got time – just start to move more than usual; avoid the lift, take the stairs
- Feel too tired – exercise will help you feel more energetic
- Can't really be bothered – why not? Find out the real reason; this is a lame excuse!
- Feel you're too old – whatever your age you will benefit from improving your fitness. Just choose the right type, level and frequency of exercise to meet your needs
- Haven't got anything to wear – don't confuse exercise with fashion. Many activities only require loose comfortable clothing. But do pay attention to your footwear. It should be comfortable, affordable and appropriate for the activity you've chosen

WHICH EXCUSE DO YOU USE?

Perhaps you:

- Have a bad back. Find out exactly what's wrong with your back; then seek advice on choosing an appropriate activity to strengthen the weakness you suffer from
- Think it's boring. There are many ways to improve your fitness; choose one that you enjoy
- Think you'll start when you've lost some weight. Together with a balanced diet, exercise can help you to lose weight. Don't wait to lose weight before you start to exercise

There is no real excuse for not improving your fitness. Start now. Don't be over-ambitious. Feel the benefits.

LOOK AT IT THIS WAY

Think about how you feel when you're stressed.

Would it help if you could:

- Take your mind off things?
- Release tension?
- Feel better about yourself?
- Sleep more soundly?
- Clear your mind and relax?
- Feel more energetic?

Exercise gives you all these things. Try it.

FOOD FOR THOUGHT

You would never consciously put the wrong fuel in your car. Nor would you expect your car to run well on poor quality fuel or to run without fuel. Why then do you expect your body to function with the wrong type of fuel, poor quality fuel or no fuel at all?

Because your digestive system slows down and more acid is produced in the stomach when you're under pressure, it's even more important to be conscious about what you eat and when.

CHECK THOSE HABITS

If when under pressure you...

- ...drink more coffee, try decaffeinated. Better still, drink water
- ...smoke more, try asking colleagues to help you cut down. Buy something special with the money you save. Do something constructive with the time you save (moving away from your immediate area of work in order to smoke means that each cigarette takes at least 15 minutes out of your day)
- ...use alcohol to relax, try relaxing in other ways: take some exercise, do something with friends or family; spend time on a hobby

CHECK THOSE HABITS

If when under pressure you...

- ...just grab the nearest thing to eat, try to plan ahead. It will increase your chances of eating the right food and release you from the worry of where the next meal's coming from
- ...skip lunch because you're too busy, try taking a short break to eat something. Paradoxically, taking a break will improve your concentration. You will work better
- ...eat more comfort foods, try eating figs, dates or other dried fruit when you need something sweet. Whilst chocolate and other comfort foods may give you a temporary lift, a short time later, you will feel worse than before
- ...end up having to eat late in the evening, choose something light and easy to digest

ARE YOU TENSE OR RELAXED?

When you're stressed your muscles will be tensed in readiness for action. Unless released, this tension becomes a source of discomfort.
Your:

- Head thumps and you can't think straight
- Eyes are sore and tired
- Body aches

The way to release this tension is through relaxation.

ARE YOU TENSE OR RELAXED?

Be aware of the tensions in your muscles when you're at work. Release them.

- Are your legs crossed tightly? Place your feet flat on the floor
- Is your brow furrowed? 'Smooth' it.
- Where is your tongue? Release it to the floor of your mouth
- Return your shoulders to their natural position

Doing something that really makes you laugh also works well. When did you last laugh?

RELAXATION FOR THE EYES

Working at a computer screen or VDU console, reading for long periods, working in very bright or very dim lighting can strain your eyes. Straining your eyes can lead to sore eyes, irritability, headaches and fatigue. Regularly relaxing your eyes with the following technique will help to reduce the strain.

Read through the following steps several times to familiarise yourself with them. Then try the whole exercise.

1. Sit with your head squarely on your shoulders and widen your eyes as much as you can.
2. Keep your head still and raise your eyes to look towards the ceiling. Hold this position for a slow count of 5.
3. Now roll your eyes slowly round to your right. Focus on something and hold it for a slow count of 5.
4. Keeping your head still, roll your eyes down, focus and hold for a slow count of 5.
5. Now roll your eyes to the left, focus and hold for a slow count of 5.
6. Roll your eyes upwards again and repeat in the other direction.
7. Finally close your eyes, let your head and shoulders relax and rest for a few moments.

RELAXING COMPLETELY

Take some time out at home and try to relax completely. Read through the steps below several times to familiarise yourself with them. Now put them into practice:

- Take the phone off the hook; switch your mobile phone off; tell your family that you don't want to be disturbed
- Lie down on a bed or the floor with your feet apart and palms facing upwards
- If you do need to support your head, use a slim pillow – the flatter you are the better
- Close your eyes and, starting from your feet, work your way around your body, focusing on each part, making sure it is relaxed before moving on to the next part
- When you first do this, your mind will wander; don't worry because with practice your mind will wander less and relaxation will be achieved more easily

Once you start to experience the benefits of relaxation try other ways such as massage, yoga, visualisation, meditation, the Alexander Technique. Find a class to go to or use some of the many books, CDs, DVDs etc available to help you.

THE VALUE OF SUPPORT

When you're under pressure the support of others is invaluable. Talking your situation through can help to:

- Clarify your thoughts
- 'Get it off your chest'
- Put things in perspective
- Sort out real from imagined issues
- Give you a different perspective
- Reduce the sense of isolation that pressure can generate

Others may be a source of guidance, direction or information; they may motivate, inspire or renew your enthusiasm. Maybe you know this, but you still don't seek their help because:

- You don't want to appear unable to cope
- You're concerned that asking for help is seen as a weakness
- Your request for support might be refused

The solution is to know how to ask, when to ask and who to ask.

ASKING FOR HELP

1. How to ask

- State your concern. Be factual, be specific: 'I'm concerned about the increase in my workload, since we reorganised the department'. Avoid dramatisation: 'I've got work coming at me from all sides. I just don't know where to turn next. I'm at my wit's end'
- Say what you want. Do you want guidance, an opinion, inspiration, a listening ear? Remember, it's support you're seeking; you should not expect others to solve your problems
- Ask when it would be convenient. Showing respect for someone else's time reduces the chances of an outright refusal of your request

2. When to ask

Sooner rather than later. If you leave it too long, both asking for and giving support becomes more difficult.

ASKING FOR HELP

3. Who to ask

Think about what you want and then ask the most appropriate person. Consider asking associates, colleagues, seniors, people outside the organisation.

It's unreasonable to expect one person to provide all your support so build yourself a network of supporters. The most effective networks are those that provide a balance of give and take. If you support others, they are more ready to return the favour when you're in need.

Plan time to build and maintain rapport with your contacts. Being in touch with them only when you need help makes a weak network.

FINDING TIME TO ADAPT

Adapting your lifestyle so that you're more resilient to the pressures at work may take time. Time is something that you might not have when you're under pressure, so think about focusing on something that:

- **Creates time:** How much time do you spend in front of the TV flicking from channel to channel, hoping that there will be something to entertain you? Try watching just one programme less in a week. You'll free up an hour. What will you do with that hour?
- **Doesn't take time:** If time is a real pressure for you at work, stop wearing a watch at weekends. Try it. Eat when you're hungry. Go to bed when you're tired. Ignore the time. Take the pressure of time right out of your life. It makes a difference

Have you noticed that you can always make time for the things that you really want to do? Might lack of time be an 'excuse'? Try changing your perception of either the task, or the time you think is available. It might be the only change you need to make.

GETTING STARTED

Making changes to your lifestyle can be challenging. Use these tips to get you started:

- Be realistic; start with something small and build on it
- See the solutions, not the obstacles
- Don't make too many changes at once or changes that are too big
- Make a commitment to yourself; write reminders and actions in your diary
- Re-live your achievements; make notes of your progress at the end of each week and re-read them
- Accept that you're human; even if your resolve occasionally weakens, stick with it
- Create a reward system for yourself
- Start now; get results – tomorrow may be too late

GETTING RESULTS

THE THREE ESSENTIALS

Managing stress at work is easier said than done.

To get results you need to:

- Recognise stress
- Know how to apply first aid (what to do in the short-term)
- Aim to prevent rather than cure (a long-term view)

CHOOSE TO RECOGNISE IT

Stress is a downward spiral. If you choose to ignore it:

- You become less able to cope
- The problems get worse
- The pressures increase

As a consequence:

- You suffer more stress
- The situation becomes more complex
- Seeking help becomes more difficult
- Getting back to 'norm' requires excessive amounts of time and effort

Do you have plenty of time and effort to spare?
What shape are you in? Can you afford to be stressed?

WHAT SIGNS WILL YOU LOOK FOR?

The quicker you recognise stress, the easier it is to manage. Nip it in the bud.

What signs will you look for?

Consider physical, mental, emotional and behavioural signs.

What might you see, hear or feel?

What's the earliest warning signal your body gives you?

Is it always the same one?

MENTAL FIRST AID

THEORY

Think about it.

Your body is giving you signals that you're stressed.

Why?

Because you've triggered the fight or flight response.

Why?

Because you perceived a situation as a threat or a challenge.

Thinking about the situation in a different way can check the downward spiral of stress.

MENTAL FIRST AID

PRACTICE

Try turning your mind to something else:

- Daydream for a few moments
- Use self-talk ('I won't get angry, it's not worth it; I'll just state my case again, calmly')
- Think how much worse the situation could be
- Keep an open mind (you're reacting badly to what you've just overheard; resolve to keep an open mind until you've established the facts)
- Check your attitude – is it positive?

You have the mental power to check the fight or flight response. Use it.

PHYSICAL FIRST AID

THEORY

When you perceive a threat or challenge, your body automatically goes into a state of alert.

Ignoring these signs means that you are in a permanent state of preparation.

The body's natural instinct is to go on trying to adapt under increasing pressure. Unless you stop it, your body will eventually break down.

Making a physical change can help your body revert to its norm.

PHYSICAL FIRST AID

PRACTICE

How is your body responding?

- If your breathing has become shallow, breathe slowly and deeply
- If your body is tensed, release the gripped muscles
- If you're slumped or slouched, sit or stand tall

Try it. It makes you feel different, doesn't it?

Can you physically walk away from the situation? Can you quite literally take a break?

Smile. Do it now. Feeling stupid doing it? Make your smile wider. Laugh at yourself. Feel different? Yes, the pressure's still there, but with that small action you've given the signal for your body to return to norm which is what first aid is all about. The sooner you apply it, the quicker you'll see results.

SCEPTICAL ABOUT FIRST AID?

Why?

Stress is caused by what happens in your mind and your body. It starts with a thought that turns into a physical response.

The way to stop it is to counter that thought and check that response.

You have a choice. You can choose to:

- Think and respond in a way that will **increase** your stress

  OR

- Think and respond in a way that will **reduce** your stress

BUT ISN'T FIRST AID DIFFICULT?

Thinking and responding in a way that will reduce stress can be difficult when you're under pressure. Positive thoughts and positive actions are often the last things on your mind.

But unless you think positive and act positive, you'll simply spiral downwards.

You are the only one who can break that spiral. No one else can do it for you. You may not have full control over the pressures around you, but you do have full control over your thoughts and responses. You can choose to think and respond negatively. You can choose to think and respond positively.

THINKING POSITIVELY

Thinking positively will make you more positive. It becomes a self-fulfilling prophecy.

When you need to apply first aid try to:

- Push negative thoughts away as soon as they come into your mind
- Avoid people who are negative and destructive
- Focus on something positive to occupy your mind
- Think about known, proven facts only
- Be objective
- Use a supportive mental mantra ('I will...'; 'I am...'; etc)
- Remind yourself that everything is relative
- Avoid reading things into a situation
- Stay rational
- Focus on what you've achieved (even when it feels like nothing, there will always be something)

DON'T make excuses. Take action. Get results. Use first aid techniques to regain control.

PREVENTION RATHER THAN CURE

THEORY

While first aid has a vital role to play in managing your stress at work, the fact that you need to apply it means that you are already experiencing stress. You've already triggered the fight or flight response.

Each time you trigger the response, you put your body under a greater strain. In your bid to handle the pressures you're under, you turn a blind eye to your body's signals. You fail to see that your performance has become impaired. You push your body too far. It gives you aches and pains, ulcers and heart attacks. It breaks down.

Where stress is concerned, prevention is preferable to cure.

PREVENTION RATHER THAN CURE

PRACTICE

To prevent stress you need to stop triggering the fight or flight response.

How many times in a normal working day do you unwittingly initiate it?

- An accident on the route to work means you arrive late
- Your colleague is sick, so now you have to fill in
- The phone rings incessantly
- Everyone wants the job done yesterday
- The boss wants to see you **now**
- Your 'to do' list remains untouched

The aim of stress management is to reduce the number of times you trigger the fight or flight response. It requires certain skills.

PREVENTION SKILLS

Learning not to trigger the fight or flight response requires a combination of skills. These skills may be:

- **Mental** Adjusting your perspective; using positive self-talk
- **Physical** Relaxing; improving your fitness
- **Organisational** Balancing the workload; making more of your time
- **Behavioural** Being assertive; managing conflict

Stress is an individual's response to pressure. What skills do you need to prevent stress? Use the pages in the 'Your Thoughts' and 'Your Responses' sections to give you ideas.

SCEPTICAL ABOUT PREVENTION?

Why?

- **Because you've read the book, seen the film, attended the training course?** Maybe you know about prevention skills in theory. Maybe from time to time you even put them into practice. But do you do it consistently? Prevention skills are about thoughts and responses that you use naturally in the course of your work. They're habits
- **Because you haven't got time?** There's no doubt that learning to prevent stress takes time. But do you have the time to recover from stress-related illnesses? Can you afford to be off work?

SCEPTICAL ABOUT PREVENTION?

Why?

- **Because it sounds like hard work?**
  Breaking old habits and developing new ones does involve effort.
  But what's the alternative? As the saying goes:

> 'If you always do what you've always done, you'll always get what you've always got.'

Being sceptical about prevention skills will only add to your pressure.
If you have concerns, try looking at them in a different light.

CONCERNED ABOUT TIME?

If you're concerned about the time that adopting prevention skills will take, remember that:

- Prevention skills are about stopping as well as starting things. Find something that you need to stop doing. Free up some time. Use it to develop your stress prevention skills
- While you're fretting about it, you're actually wasting time. Stop fretting. Think and do something positive
- When your prevention skills have become habits, you will actually have more time

MAKE THE RIGHT CHANGES

Developing prevention skills means making changes. Before initiating a change, make sure it's worth it. Some changes turn out to be additional sources of pressure.

Avoid:

- The flavour of the month change:
  Last month it was 'The Grapefruit Diet', this month it's 'Bananas and Pears.'
  You will fail to make progress

- The hot air change:
  You talk constantly about getting a new job, but don't even start the process.
  You will lose face

- The half-baked change:
  You stop smoking, but start over-eating.
  You will lose your self-esteem

MAKE THE RIGHT CHANGES

Avoid:

- The cart before the horse change:
  You enter yourself for the local marathon, and then take up jogging.
  You will over-stretch yourself
- The damp squib change:
  You manage two days with no coffee, but now you're back on the usual drip feed.
  You will become irritable – and that's a sure sign of stress

All these changes increase the pressure you're under. Only make changes that reduce your pressure.

PLANNING WORTHWHILE CHANGES

Ask yourself four questions to ensure that you don't even begin to make a change until you've established that it will be worthwhile.

Consider:

1. What you do now.
2. What you want to do.
3. How you're going to do it.

Then ask yourself:

4. Does this feel worthwhile?

Adjust your plan until the answer to question 4 is a resounding YES. Only then will you get results.

STRESS IN YOUR ORGANISATION

YOUR ROLE & RESPONSIBILITIES

Stress is an individual's reaction to pressure. The individuals in an organisation are therefore responsible for stress at work. Everyone is responsible.

When people at work are stressed, morale is low, inefficiencies abound, mistakes are made, absenteeism rises, profits fall. When an organisation suffers from stress, it starts on the same downward spiral that we experience as individuals.

As an individual within an organisation you should take the responsibility to manage your own stress and:

- Ensure that you're not a source of pressure
- Help others who are under pressure
- Encourage a low stress culture

ARE YOU INCREASING THE PRESSURE?

We're all human. We all have faults. But have you ever considered that when you think you are...

- Working well as a team member
- Being a good leader
- Helping others

...you may actually be increasing the pressure?

BEING A SOURCE OF PRESSURE

Pressure on others is increased by:

- Being inconsistent – blowing hot and cold
- Letting people down – not doing what you said you would do
- Imposing your own values – if you work through lunch breaks and at weekends, you expect others to do this too
- Not planning – always being in a last minute rush and needing something done 'yesterday'
- Being aggressive or submissive rather than assertive
- Being unnecessarily 'loud' in a shared work area
- Taking a negative perspective
- Being possessive about equipment, work or information that others would benefit from
- Being overly competitive and always needing to 'win'
- Ignoring the feelings or needs of others
- Interrupting

Do you do any of these things? Are you a source of pressure for others?

BEING A SOURCE OF PRESSURE

Ironically, many of the things listed opposite increase the pressure on you too. Stop doing them. It will help to reduce your pressure and the pressure within your organisation.

What else do you do that might increase pressure?

Find out by talking to the people you work with. Ask them what you can stop doing to reduce pressure at work.

- **B**e prepared to take it on the chin
- **A**ct on it right away
- **C**heck that the change has reduced the pressure
- **OFF**er to do something else

If you're a source of pressure at work, **BAC**k-**OFF**.

PRESSURE IN THE TEAM

As a member of a team you are part of a group that has been formed solely for the convenience of the organisation. The only thing you may have in common with other team members is a set of goals. How do you behave in your team?

Do you:

- Work as an individual rather than a team member?
- Withhold information from others in the team?
- Break into sub-groups rather than work together?
- Indulge in win/lose conflicts within the team?
- Pursue your own agenda rather than the goals of the team?
- Fail to pull your weight?

If you are doing any of these things you are creating pressure for yourself and others. Stop. If others are behaving in this way, confront them and resolve it.

WHEN YOU'RE IN CHARGE

When you are in charge of others at work, reduce the pressure on yourself by:

- Taking 'time off' from your responsibilities; leave work and leave it behind
- Delegating – in the short-term it may seem time consuming but in the long-term it's liberating
- Creating time to think and plan, to step away, rather than do
- Accepting that you will not always be liked by everyone
- Having a degree of humility

While the nature of your job may not enable you to do all of these things all of the time, try doing at least one of them every day.

BEING RESPONSIBLE FOR OTHERS

When you're responsible for others at work reduce pressure on them by:

- **Motivating with a carrot rather than a stick**

  Both the stick and the carrot will increase pressure. But the stick is more likely to be seen as a threat. As such it's more likely to trigger stress. Try not to use it

- **Making any criticism constructive**

  Be specific. State the problem in terms of the behaviour not the person. Agree a course of action

- **Avoiding knee jerk, dictatorial styles of management**

  Participative, open, empowering styles are generally less stressful

BEING RESPONSIBLE FOR OTHERS

When you're responsible for others at work reduce pressure on them by:

- **Encouraging a culture that reduces pressure**

  Make it acceptable to take lunch breaks and holidays. Don't make people feel guilty if they're the first to leave work. Talk openly about stress

- **Getting to know them**

  Learn to recognise their individual signs of stress and what might cause them stress. Their signs, concerns and values may be very different from your own

- **Making it easy for them to ask you for help**

  Avoid the macho attitude of 'if you can't stand the heat get out of the kitchen'. The longer a situation is left before it is aired, the more complex it may become. It may, therefore, be more difficult to resolve

WHEN YOU'RE ASKED FOR HELP

When someone asks you for help they're already under pressure. Try not to increase it further.

DON'T:

- ✗ Dismiss their concern – 'You're probably worrying over nothing'
- ✗ Give your opinion unless you're asked for it
- ✗ Question their actions – 'Why on earth did you do that?'
- ✗ Be judgmental – 'I certainly don't think you should have...'
- ✗ Hijack the conversation so they can't get a word in
- ✗ Relay your own life history – 'That sounds like when I was at...'
- ✗ Give sympathy – give empathy instead

Doing any of these things will probably:

- Leave someone feeling worse than before
- Increase the pressure they're under
- Discourage them from seeking help in the future

HOW TO HELP OTHERS

When you're giving help to others:

DO:

1. Let them speak

✔ Give them time; don't hurry them; be prepared for silence
✔ Encourage them with open questions – How? When? Where? Who? What?
✔ Extend their comments – 'Tell me more about...'
✔ Use supportive statements – 'I see...' 'Okay' 'That's interesting...'

2. Listen to them

✔ Use body language to show that you're listening – eye contact, nodding, raising of eyebrows
✔ Show that you are following by saying 'mm', 'right' 'uhha'
✔ Reflect back what's been said – 'So you feel that...'
✔ Check that you understand – 'So your main concern is...'

HOW TO HELP OTHERS

When you're giving help to others, **DO:**

3. **Help them to help themselves**
   By doing this they will learn how to handle similar situations and cope better in the future. Help them to:

✔ Establish what the real problem is
✔ Explore different perspectives
✔ Seek solutions by asking 'what if' questions

4. **Follow-up**

✔ Find out how they're getting on. Check that they're making progress.

Important

- DON'T try to solve their problems for them or 'rescue' them
- DO consider getting them to read this book
- If you feel that someone needs more than first level assistance with stress management, encourage them to seek the guidance of a fully trained stress counsellor or therapist

ENCOURAGING A LOW-STRESS CULTURE

Everyone in an organisation contributes towards its culture. To create a low-stress culture it is important to:

- Take responsibility; don't be part of a blame culture
- Talk about stress; make it acceptable rather than taboo
- Avoid linking your self-esteem to your earning power or holding promotion as an emblem of success
- Learn as much as you can about stress and put it into practice
- Communicate, keep people informed; if you don't know, ask
- Co-operate; work together
- Give and accept support
- Learn to accept change

Stress is catching, make sure you're not the one that's spreading it.

YOUR FUTURE

Everyone experiences pressure, and pressure at work often results in stress. But it doesn't have to. While you may not have the ability to control all the pressures you face, you do have the ability to control your responses to them. Use this ability. Your relationship with stress depends on it.

About the Author

Mary Richards wrote the first edition of this book when she was a business consultant and trainer, with a background in education, international marketing and general management. Mary now combines her writing with her work as a therapist. This second edition has been written in the light of her interest in the links between the mind, the emotions, the body's structure and energy systems – and many more life experiences!

She is the author of 'The Telephone Skills Pocketbook' in this same series.

To reach Mary Richards, please contact the publisher in the first instance.

Your details

Name ______________________________

Position ______________________________

Company ______________________________

Address ______________________________

____

____

Telephone ______________________________

Fax ______________________________

E-mail ______________________________

VAT No. (EC companies) ______________________________

Your Order Ref ______________________________

Please send me:

			No. copies
The	Stress	Pocketbook	
The		Pocketbook	
The		Pocketbook	
The		Pocketbook	

Order by Post

MANAGEMENT POCKETBOOKS LTD

LAUREL HOUSE, STATION APPROACH,
ALRESFORD, HAMPSHIRE SO24 9JH UK

Order by Phone, Fax or Internet

Telephone: +44 (0)1962 735573
Facsimile: +44 (0)1962 733637
Email: sales@pocketbook.co.uk
Web: www.pocketbook.co.uk

Customers in USA should contact:

Management Pocketbooks
2427 Bond Street, University Park, IL 60466
Telephone: 866 620 6944 Facsimile: 708 534 7803
Email: mp.orders@ware-pak.com
Web: www.managementpocketbooks.com